Australian Poems that would Boggle a BULL!

Philip R. Rush

Published by Philip R. Rush Pty. Ltd. ACN 082 969 882
224 Sunny Hills Road
Glen Huon   Tasmania 7109
Telephone (03) 6266 6331
www.philiprush.com.au

Copyright © text Philip R. Rush 1997
Copyright © illustrations Megan L. Rush 1997

1st Edition June 1997 2500 copies
2nd Impression August 1997 2500 copies
3rd Impression December 1997 3000 copies
4th Impression January 1999 2000 copies
5th Impression October 1999 3000 copies
6th Impression March 2001 3000 copies
7th Impression November 2002 3000 copies
8th Impression February 2004 2500 copies

All rights reserved.
No part of this publication may be produced, stored in a retrieval system or
transmitted in any form or by any means, electronic, mechanical, photocopying,
recording or otherwise, without the prior written permission of Philip R. Rush, or,
in the case of the illustrations, Megan L. Rush.

Printed and bound by The Monotone Art Printers Pty Ltd,
Argyle Street, Hobart Tasmania

ISBN 0 646 32172 2

To my family, for their forbearance in listening to, and creative criticism of, all the poems in this book; and to Jim McCarter for his assistance with the title.

CONTENTS

MURPHY'S LAW ON THE FARM

*(Murphy's Law - "Whatever can go wrong, will go wrong."
Not only at home, but in the workplace, be it in the city office,
or out on the farm!)*

I'd heard about this Murphy's Law from mates o' mine in town,
Everythin' was going wrong, and they were pretty down;
They said that I was lucky to be livin' on the farm,
Where life is free o' trouble, and clear of any harm.

Now I know it sounds like whingein', but I'm only statin' facts,
But the boys had got their info from the wrong side of the tracks.
"This Murphy's Law yer talks about, in town it's just a fad,
We blokes have lived with it for years, since Grandpa was a lad."

"Yer reckon you got problems, but yer dunno you're alive,
Working fancy hours inside from half-past eight to five:
The weather doesn't bother yer; and when somethin' isn't right,
Yer get a flamin' tradesman in to fix it overnight."

"Now 'ere, o' course, it's different, we work from dawn to dark,
And, when we're needin' quiet, the dogs begin to bark.
And, when the grass is ready, we cut it down for hay,
Which, as every farmer knows, brings rain the followin' day."

"I stock me farm with cattle, for beef is lookin' fine,
But, when I goes to sell 'em, the market's in decline.
So back to sheep I changes, but, stone the bloomin' crows,
The Asians 'ave stopped buyin', and down the prices goes."

"When I want to do some ploughin', me tractor doesn't start:
When I want to split some fenceposts, me chainsaw falls apart:
When I need a spot of rainfall, all I get is wretched drought:
But, when a dry spell's wanted, there's always rain about!"

I planned the lambin' late this year, to miss the cold and sleet,
But then I gets a string of frosts instead of gentle heat.
Me pastures need improvement, and clover gets me vote,
And then, when springtime comes around, me cattle suffer bloat!"

"Don't talk to me of Murphy's Law, I know it all to well,
And every farmer what I knows has similar tales to tell:
Whatever can go wrong, they say, will go wrong, for sure,
But, on the farm, when things go wrong, they go wrong even more!"

TIME

(I guess a calendar is useful, and a watch is necessary at times, but farming folk are more used to thinking about time a little differently to city folk. This poem came about when a dear old lady had invited my wife and me to dinner. She had a host of stories to tell, and, when I asked as to the time of year a certain one occurred, she didn't reply with a date, but with "At raspberry pickin' time.)

I visited me neighbour, Pete, just the other day,
He told me he had organised to take a trip away.
I said, "And when you're goin' on this fancy holiday?"
And he replied, "At raspberry pickin' time."

I saw Jack Kelly's daughter, Kate, along with husband Jim;
She looked very motherly, and he looked pretty trim.
I said, "And when's the baby due? And is it her or him?"
And Jack replied, "He's due at harvest time."

I hadn't seen old Tommy Kite for near a year or so,
And then I bumped into his son who put me in the know.
"I guess yer heard," he said to me, "Dad died some months ago;
A week or two from apple blossom time."

Cousin Don phoned yesterday about a half past two,
Invitin' me to come and stay, and bring the family, too.
I said, "Right-o; and what time's best to come and visit you?"
"I guess," he said, "just after shearing time."

Tim and Alice down the road, they run a herd of cows,
And Alice asked us round for tea, for they are mates of ours.
"And when should I arrive?" I says. "Me and all the girls?"
She answered me, "Come after milkin' time."

Us country folk don't always work by calendars and dates:
It's seasons, plants, and animals, is how we operate,
And heat and cold, and frost and rain, it's them our work dictates;
And now I'm off because it's dinner-time!

THE DEAD QUOLL

(Tasmania has an abundance of wild life, beautiful wild life. Possums, wallabies, bandicoots, potoroos, pademelons, echidnas, and quolls being but a selection. As a result of such abundance, the roads are littered with dead animals, some of which bring more distress than others!)

'Twas only a quoll, not endangered or rare;
The corpse on the road with its unseeing stare.
The dark, dusty form, all spotted with white,
Would no longer hunt by the moon's yellow light.
Its rusty-red tail with beautiful fur,
Pathetically waved in the wind's gentle stir.
Rabbit or possum, lizard or snake,
Lying dead on the road don't make my heart ache.
And, 'though many beasts on our highway must die,
The death of a quoll brings a tear to my eye.

FERGY

(The little grey Ferguson tractor celebrated its fiftieth anniversary in 1996. An icon on the farm, both in Australia and overseas, this hard-working little tractor was as reliable a machine as one could wish to find. I was one of many country folk who learnt to drive a tractor sitting on the sprung steel seat of the little grey Fergy. Although now mostly superseded by bigger and more comfortable tractors, one can still find on many farms today, either working, or stored in a shed, the little grey Ferguson tractor.)

It stands in the old machinery shed,
Between the ute and a rusty bed,
And liberally covered in spiders' web,
The little grey Ferguson tractor.

I reckon it's forty years, or more,
Since Dad purchased it, but Im not quite sure;
And I can't recall what he had before
Our little grey Ferguson tractor.

On the left-hand side there's a toolbox still
With some bolts inside, and a broken drill.
And her name-plate's there, above the grille
Of the little grey Ferguson tractor.

The two front tyres are narrow and worn,
And most of the tread from the back two's gone:
Covered in dust, she looks quite forlorn,
Our little grey Ferguson tractor.

For years the Fergy was all they had
As they worked the farm - just Mum and Dad;
And I learnt to drive, when still a lad,
On the little grey Ferguson tractor.

As my father sat on the steel-sprung seat
In the winter's frost, or the summer's heat,
She never faltered, or missed a beat,
The little grey Ferguson tractor.

After years of work she's stored away,
Dreaming of many a yesterday:
For she's played the part that she had to play,
The little grey Ferguson tractor.

BLACK COCKATOOS

*(Black cockatoos are magnificent birds, and a familiar
sight in many areas throughout our land.)*

Above the gum trees gentle sigh,
I heard a long and mournful cry,
Black cockatoos were passing by.

Looking up, I saw the two
Silhouetted against the blue:
I watched in awe as on they flew.

Made by our great Creator's hand,
Across the ages they have spanned,
Ancient birds of ancient land.

JUST DESSERTS

(A story I was told many years ago by a farmer in the Wimmera. He told me that the story was true, but, having heard it in other places, I somehow doubt its veracity!)

Me neighbour, Peter Murphy, has a henhouse full of chooks,
And, without a doubt, his wife Elaine's our district's greatest cook:
Sponges, biscuits, tarts and pies, she bakes them one and all,
And they are always first to go at every local stall.

But, sadly, it's not all the eggs go into things she bakes,
The Murphy's farm's infested with a multitude of snakes!
They all enjoy a feed of eggs, and, when no-one is around,
They wriggle underneath the gate without the slightest sound.

The hens kick up a din, of course, but help arrives too late;
When Pete turns up, the snakes have gone,
      far from the chook-house gate.
He's caught a straggler once or twice, but, till last Friday week,
The snakes around the Murphy's farm were on a winning streak!

On that day, a snake turned up, a monstrous, shining black;
So big it was, it found it hard to wriggle through the crack.
It grabbed an egg and swallowed it, then turned to go away,
But Pete had come to gather eggs far earlier that day.

The big black snake retreated through the wire-netting fence,
The hole was hardly large enough, the snake was so immense!
When only halfway through it stopped, this snake as black as coal,
The egg he'd swallowed caused a bulge far bigger than the hole!

He struggled hard to free himself, making such a racket,
That Peter quickly found it, but, unwilling to attack it,
He fed the snake another egg, which now ran out of luck,
For it, with bulges either side, was well and truly stuck!

The captured snake writhed back and forth, but all to no avail,
Its head remained outside the pen, and inside lashed the tail!
When Pete arrived next morning, he had the final laugh,
So frantic had the writhing been, the snake was cut in half!

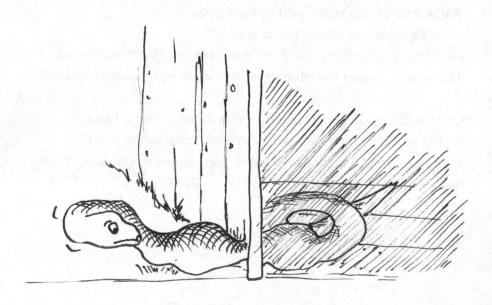

SPIDERS

(There seems to be in most of us an innate fear of one or more of the various creatures that like to share our houses and yards with us. For some it is snakes, for others moths and other 'flapping' insects, and for some it is spiders. Where there is a 'spider-hater', there is also often a rescuer, the person whose job it is to remove all such offending beasties from the house!)

In the rhyme of Miss Muffett a whacking great spider
Came up to the lassie, and sat down beside her;
And, surprise of surprises, and wonder of wonders,
    it frightened Miss Muffett away!
Now, over the centuries, since that poem was written,
All manner of spiders have frightened and bitten
Lassies and ladies, and children and adults, and continue
    to do so today.

When I was a youngster, I found that my mother,
Along with my father, and also my brother,
Had no love of spiders, in fact, found them scary, and
    tried to keep out of their way.
Whenever a spider was seen in our dwelling,
It triggered some over-emotional yelling,
And I would come running to rescue the person by taking
    the spider away.

I would pick up the spider with hand or with paper,
But, if I was tardy, I might have to scrape her
From the wall, or the floor, for someone had squashed
    her with a swat, a shoe, or a tray.

I didn't like this, for I felt for each spider,
And was sorry that life had now been denied her;
A feeling I have, although somewhat lessened, with
        spiders I deal with today.

If my wife saw a spider, when we were first married,
I would see that the creature was carefully carried
Outside to the garden and placed in the shadows, and
        there, for a while, it'd stay.
But once my wife knew that I rescued each spider,
The primeval fear that was somewhere inside her,
Insisted that spiders that trespassed upon us be
        sentenced that very same day!

So now, when a spider unwisely encroaches,
I duly remember my spouse's reproaches,
Who told me the spiders I carefully rescued returned on
        the following day!
Over the years my emotions have hardened,
No longer the spiders return to the garden,
But yet at each spider's decreed execution I still feel a
        hint of dismay!

THE HUNTSMAN SPIDER

*(Common in both city and country, and often called 'triantelope',
and rarely loved!)*
The huntsman spider, hairy creature,
Has one, at least, redeeming feature;
Although she'd win no beauty prize,
She is adept at catching flies!

THE LETTER BOX

*(Those of us living in rural Australia often have an RMB or RSD address.
That means we have a Road Mail Box, or Road Side Delivery, and often
these boxes can be seen in a cluster at the end of a country lane or road. On
shifting to Tasmania I needed a new one, and this is its story!)*

We had to have a letter-box, we're going RSD,
But what to use, or make, or buy, was really troubling me.
A metal or a plastic drum? A fancy wooden sort?
Or purchase a commercial type, one like my neighbour bought?

But then I thought of all the logs that lie about my land;
A hollow length of one of those put on a fancy stand
Would make an ideal letter-box, and not that hard to do;
I took my chainsaw down the hill to cut the timber through.

I found a dry and hollow log, and cut a decent length,
But the wood was old and brittle, with insufficient strength;
For, when I dropped it on the ground, it promptly fell apart,
And so I found another log, and made another start.

It wasn't quite as hollow as the one I'd cut before,
So I used my chainsaw carefully to hollow it some more;
I wasn't quite precise enough, and, as the opening grew,
I cut too closely to the edge, and watched it split in two!

Third time lucky, so it's said, and so it was with me,
I cut a knotty two-foot length as solid as could be.
I hollowed it a little bit, then took it round to Jim:
At woodwork I'm a novice in comparison with him!

I used the chainsaw once again, with Jim my able guide,
And soon the log was well and truly hollowed out inside.
And then the fledgling letter-box we carried to his shed,
Where Jim was in his element - I let him have his head!

He shaped the timbers for the back to match the log precisely;
The door, with twin brass hinges too, he fitted very nicely.
And all the cracks were siliconed to keep the weather out,
We'd have a fancy letter-box - no shadow of a doubt!

But, mind you, there was more to do, the things that mattered most,
The platform for the letter-box, and all-important post.
I thought that fifteen minutes more were all that we would need,
But Jim would not be hurried, he's perfectionist indeed!

But now the box is finished; beside the road it stands:
There's not another like it, it's both unique and grand!
It keeps our letters safe and dry in weather wild or bleak;
But what I thought would take us hours had taken us a week!

BUSHFIRE!

(One of the ever-present dangers throughout much of Australia in the summer and autumn, the bushfire has taken an enormous toll in both urban and rural communities over the years. Whenever one is burning within cooee of one's house or property, it's behaviour is carefully monitored.)

It's not the scent of our new-mown hay,
There's a hint of smoke in the air today.

The brassy sky at dusk last night
Forewarned of heat at morning light.

The sun arose with a fiery glow,
Reflecting red on the melting snow.

An apprehension, a slight unease,
Grows with the strengthening northerly breeze.

We check the pump and the knapsack sprays,
As the sun is dimmed by the smoky haze.

The hours creep by as we watch and wait,
While the radio keeps us up to date.

"Out of control, and spreading fast;
Stay indoors till the danger's past."

A spark of hope - as every eye
See clouds appear in the western sky.

Late afternoon, and the clouds obscure
The sun from each watching, anxious viewer.

As the day drifts on to smoky night,
The northern hills are glowing bright.

At last! A sound to relieve the strain!
The roof is drumming to heavy rain.

The danger's gone - and the sense of dread!
A collective sigh, and it's off to bed!

A PARADOX

(Written while sitting enjoying the morning sunshine high above the Huon Valley in Tasmania)

A quite exquisite butterfly flew past on dainty wings:
I felt the sense of wonderment that such creation brings.
A moment later it was dead, caught by a passing bird,
A beauty instantly destroyed, a paradox absurd.
Nature's creativity is wondrous to behold,
But oft her seeming cruelty makes my blood run cold!

THE OLD GRINDSTONE

(We may often see something that will remind us of days long past, and this old grindstone I found behind a shed was no exception).

I found it down behind the shed,
Beside a rusting iron bed;
A grindstone, mounted on a frame,
If one could give it such a name.

The wooden frame was warped and grey,
And had been left to rot away.
But there, defiantly, it stood,
For it was made of sturdy wood.

The ageing legs were shaky now,
But managed still to stand, somehow.
The lichen-covered, battered stone,
Would never more a sickle hone.

I helped my Grandpa once or twice
To use this derelict device
When it was in a working state;
I guess I was but seven or eight.

The handle now was rusty brown,
I couldn't even turn it round:
But fifty years ago I could,
For then it functioned as it should.

Although I was a little boy,
I would always quite enjoy
Helping Pa - I'd turn the wheel,
And watch the sparks fly from the steel.

Sickle, fern-hook, scythe, and spade,
Axe, or knife with blunted blade;
All were ground with special care,
While I turned the handle there.

When the job was at an end,
Pa a helping hand would lend:
The wheel's momentum was too great
For a little boy of eight.

Still behind the shed it stands,
No longer used by calloused hands.
And there it stays, while frame will last,
Reminding me of days long past.

STRENGTH

(One can only be impressed at the strength shown by many of the fungi as they push their way upwards!)

Slowly heaves the dark, moist soil,
Then fractures, to reveal
A fungus, busy at its toil,
As tough as any steel.

OLD JOE

Old Joe was in his nineties, and now without a wife,
She died a year last Thursday, it cut him like a knife.
For sixty years and longer, they'd farmed their bit of land,
And, even in their eighties, they were sinewy and tanned.

But the burden of the years tells on e'en the fittest folk;
When Joe was nearly ninety he suffered from a stroke.
It wasn't all that serious, and didn't cause much harm,
But, though it nearly broke their hearts, they had to sell the farm.

They had no-one to leave it to, both their sons were dead,
John had drowned when he was twelve, and war took brother Fred.
So Joe and Ethel sold the farm and shifted into town,
But both were lost without the bush, and couldn't settle down.

A few, short months and Ethel died, a victim of the 'flu,
And Joe was telling me last week he wished he'd caught it, too.
"What say, old friend," I said to him, to bring a bit of cheer,
"We spend some hours tomorrow on a farm not far from here."

He brightened up quite lively, and said he'd love to come.
I fixed it with my farming mate, and gave him all the drum.
'Twas eight o'clock when we arrived, and Joe spent all the day
Wandering around the farm, and smelling new-mown hay.

He called the dogs, he patted sheep, and felt their greasy wool,
He said, "The season's good, I see, and all your dams are full."
He reminisced for hours and hours, and hardly stopped to eat;
When nightfall came he'd worn us out; my mate and I were beat!

'Twas after dark when Joe and I drove back to town that night,
He went inside, and went to bed, and died by morning light.
And when I went back round again to Joe, my cobber's, place,
The neighbour said he died in peace, a smile upon his face.

MICE

There seems a lot of mice about;
Maybe the rain has washed them out.
The cats, when hunting in the yard,
Have caught a few that were off-guard.
Now I don't mind the odd grey mouse,
Unless, of course, they're in our house!

OLD ROVER

(It is difficult to imagine a more Australian scene than a drover, or farmer, with his dog. Old Rover was my uncle's favourite dog during the nineteen-fifties, a tan-and-white kelpie cross. I remember, Old Rover sleeping in a patch of sunlight at the back of the farmhouse, while his two sons, Young Pup and Old Pup, did the work!)

Arthritic, half-blind, and going grey,
Old Rover sleeps in the sun today,
And dreams of times that have long since gone,
When he worked the stock with his master, Ron.

He recalls the years when, on nimble feet,
He'd run all day in the summer's heat,
Responding to whistles, and call "Way-back",
He'd push the stock along the track.

No bull, no ram, no sheep, no steer,
Caused Old Rover an ounce of fear.
No chance for a beast to break away,
Whether half-ton giant, or surly stray.

If Ron was doing some other job,
He'd watch, on his own, the wandering mob.
Unaided, without his master's help,
He'd control the stock with stare and yelp.

As time went by, and years rolled on,
He taught the pups for his master, Ron;
And now they work, as he sleeps in the sun,
Dreaming of years of a job well done.

THE GATEWAY

(The bane of many a farmer - the paddock gateway that never dries out, and is always a mess!)

Down in me bottom paddock, the gateway is a mess,
I suppose I'd better go and try to fix it up, I guess;
But, mind you, I have tried, at least, a dozen times before;
I really shouldn't grumble as I fix it up once more!

It's in this bit of hollow, see, and every time it rains,
No matter what I do with it, it turns to mud again!
I've filled it up with stones and bricks, I've filled it up with rocks,
I've filled it up with heavy logs, and even concrete blocks!

But all the things I've ever used have been a wretched dud,
For, somehow, they get pushed aside, or sink beneath the mud;
I've got a load of gravel here, I'll drop that in today,
But I've got a sinkin' feelin' that the hole is here to stay!

Me dog got bogged the other day while rounding up the sheep,
The look he gave, when rescued, would make a drover weep.
I lost a cow and calf last year, they sunk without a trace,
Me insurance wouldn't cover what they cost me to replace!

What's that I hear you sayin'? Move the gateway up a bit?
If I did that me dad would have an apoplectic fit!
His grand-dad put the gateway there in eighteen ninety-two,
What's good enough for Gramps, me lad, is good enough for you!

FARM SOUNDS

(When we are travelling, or are away from home for some time, we sometimes wish for a reminder of those things we find familiar and comforting.)

The lowing of cattle, the bleat of a lamb,
The chugging of pumps by the side of a dam.
The clank of the baler, the wind in the trees,
The creak of the windmill, the buzzing of bees.
The throb of the tractor, the barking of dogs,
The roar of the chainsaw, the croaking of frogs.
The call of the plover, the clucking of hens,
The crying of ravens, the chatter of wrens.
The crack of the welder, the cockatoos' screams,
The rhythmical swishing of milking machines.
Wherever I wander, wherever I roam,
Any one of these noises reminds me of home!

THE LOCAL HALL

(In many of our rural communities, the local hall was the focal point of much of the social life of the district. Many of them were known as the Mechanics Institute Hall, or, maybe, a memorial Hall. Often they were used to house the local library, and rarely a week would go by without some event taking place in the local hall. Unfortunately, with the passage of time, many local halls have fallen into disrepair, and are now seldom used).

It was built in Queen Victoria's time; it's more than a century old,
Some early settler donated the land - at least, that's what I was told.
It used to be home to a Library once, there's still some old books
      on the shelves;
There's nothing of value, they're faded and worn, but
      you're welcome to look for yourselves.

The floor's not as good as it used to be once, when a
      dance every month was the go;
The whole district would come, from oldies to kids, it kept
      us together, you know.
And parties we had for engagements and things, and for
      kids when they turned twenty-one;
My own twenty-first I remember quite well, along with
      those of my sons.

Card nights we ran to raise funds for the school, or make
      a few quid for the Hall.
And, back in the fifties, we'd square-dancing, too; old
      Timothy Wright did the call.

The wood-stove in the kitchen has long rusted out;
   my word! It used to get hot!
The four-gallon kettles have rusted out, too, and so has
   the cast-iron pot.

There's two Honour Boards that list all of the names of
   the locals who went to the Wars;
With a little gold cross besides each of the blokes who
   gave up their lives for the cause.
Some of these names bring a tear to my eye,
   for I lost quite a few of my mates,
But you never can tell, I may meet them again, when I
   pass through those heavenly gates!

The Hall was important when I was a lad, the centre of
   town, so to speak;
I reckon there used to be happenings there two or three
   times every week.
But now, apart from the Badminton Team, and perhaps
   a school concert or play,
The Hall is deserted, its future uncertain: a relic from earlier days.

THE TAWNY FROGMOUTH

Statue-like, at night he sits
In suit of sombre grey;
A sombre costume that befits
This shunner of the day.

NOT GUILTY

Once again, I've lost my glasses,
And, as every moment passes,
My impatience and my irritation grows;
I often seem to lose them
When I really need to use them;
I put them on my desk an hour ago!

And now somebody's shifted,
Or mischievously lifted,
My car keys from the hook beside the door.
They're not now where they should be,
I wonder where they could be?
I know I hung them on the hook before!

This familiar situation
Causes me intense frustration,
And it goes beyond my glasses and the keys:
Wrenches, pliers, saws and spanners,
Crowbar, shovel, files and hammers,
Seem to disappear right in front of me!

When I really should be farming,
The time wasted is alarming,
Looking round for all the little things I use.
I'm annoyed, and disapproving
Of whoever is removing
All these items, but who should I accuse?

Yesterday my wire strainer
That was next to the container,
Was no longer where it should be on the shelf.
Someone moved, or someone hid it,
But there's no-one will admit it;
I'm not guilty, for I put it back myself!

When these troubles I'm explaining,
My wife says, "Stop complaining,
You know you're an untidy sort of coot."
But, regardless what she thinks,
I put things back - "Oh! Strike me pink!
Now someone's gone and moved me wretched boots!

THE MASKED PLOVER

(A well-known bird throughout much of our land; it thrives on farmland, and its shrill, staccato call is a common sound in the country, especially at dawn and dusk, and often into the night.)

At dusk, and oft throughout the night, I hear a harsh staccato call;
And also at dawn's early light, as mountains shed their misty shawl:
The cry of plovers, sharp and shrill, with inharmonious intonation,
Reaches me upon the hill, and interrupts my contemplations.

MODERN TIMES

(Modern technology is not only a city phenomenon, it has made its presence felt in the country as well!)

My neighbour's name is Arthur Wood,
He always looks like farmers should:
Most days I see him on our track
In his pair of gumboots black;
A battered hat, a rainproof coat,
A woollen scarf around his throat;
Toughened trousers, flannel shirt,
His ancient ute is sprayed with dirt.
He stops beside the paddock fence,
And throws the hay with strength immense.
Then, climbing over wooden rails,
He cuts the twine around the bales,
And spreads the sweet and golden hay
To feed his cows each winter's day.
But then, this morning, I'll admit
That I was taken back a bit;
For, surrounded by his herd,
A rather strange event occurred.
As Arthur stood on muddy ground,
I thought I heard a ringing sound;
And soon I heard it yet again;
Then Arthur, in the drizzling rain,
Stood, soaking wet - a man alone,
And talked into his mobile 'phone!

HEARTACHE

(A sad, but not unfamiliar story).

They're old and they're tired,
And both have desired
To hand the farm onto their son.
But he's gone away,
Not wishing to stay
On the dairy farm they had begun.

For fifty years now
They've been milking cows,
And wish to retire and relax.
They cleared all the land
By tractor and hand,
And built all the fences and tracks.

The dairy and sheds
And superb garden beds
They developed with blood, sweat and tears.
But now they are worn,
Their energy gone,
As their youth with the passing of years.

They view with alarm
That their dear little farm
In the future may have to be sold.
So they struggle each day
With the milking and hay,
And the ailments afflicting the old.

So as they persist
In the rain and the mist,
In the heat, and the dawn's early light;
They hope that one day
Their grandchildren may
Do the milking each morning and night.

WHERE IS SUMMER?

(A 'not-too-warm' summer in '95-6, and the promise of similar weather in '96-7, led to this rhyme).

They tell me summer's coming, and maybe they are right,
But, judging by the forecasts I've been hearing every night,
Our winter hung about us well past the normal date,
And spring may also linger exceptionally late.

Well into November the snow is falling still,
Not only on the mountains, but on the lower hills.
And rain! We'd had our annual share by early in September,
But still it comes; and now, I'm told, we'll have a wet December!

I think, last year, the summer came for just a day or two,
Before the autumn bustled in on south-west gales that blew
For weeks on end, then winter came, with months
     of snow and frost;
And now we face the prospect of another summer lost!

CONVERSATION

(The weather, a universal topic of conversation. Whether one lives in town or country, somewhere in our daily conversation the weather will play a part.)

No matter where I shop or walk,
I often stop to have a talk.
"How are you, Bill, and how's your kids?
I see that beef is on the skids."
Bill says, in his concise reply,
"They're all fine and so am I.
And prices have gone down the drain;
And I think it's going to rain."
I say "goodbye" as Bill goes by,
And look up at a cloudless sky.

I stroll a little further on,
And meet my my next door neighbour, Don.
"Gidday!" I says, "It's been a while
Since I've seen you." He gives a smile.
"Yeah", he says, "Too much to do.
And how's your kids, and Yvonne, too?"
I go to speak, but all too slow.
Don says, "I think we'll see some snow.
The weather has been pretty bleak;
It's sure to snow sometime this week."

Don wanders off; I scratch my head,
The sun is shining overhead.
I mutter gently as I go,
"There's not a sign of rain or snow."

I head into the butcher's shop
And order steak, and mince, and chops.
The butcher says, "Is that the lot?
I think the day will turn out hot."
"Oh, I don't know," I says, and pays,
"It's one of those more pleasant days."

In supermarket, bank, or store,
I meet with folk, and talk some more.
And, in every chat we start,
The weather plays a major part.
We talk of rain, we talk of hail,
Or some unseasonable gale:
Of winter's cold, of summer's heat,
Of fog and frost, and snow and sleet.
No matter where folk meet together,
They always talk about the weather!

THE FIRE

*(Many of us have a favourite nook or cranny, maybe a shed, maybe a special
chair. High on my list is a reclining chair beside the fire.*

The rain descends from clouds of grey,
The raw wind whistles loud;
And, as it rages on its way,
Protesting trees are bowed.
I hear the weather roar and scream
Like some demonic choir:
But I sit peacefully and dream
Beside my friendly fire.

RECORDS

(Another poem about the weather. I had heard on the news that Perth had had a record of some sort. This led me to thinking about the obsession many of us have with the weather, and the various records that seem to be an inevitable consequence of such insatiable interest).

When the news I had heard
That in Perth had occurred
A hailstorm of record dimension;
I decided to go
To the weather bureau;
To learn of the facts my intention.

It was pouring with rain
As I dressed once again
For the winter and all of its rigours.
To the bureau I went,
And I asked for the gent
Who could tell me the facts and the figures.

Soon a man came to me,
And 'twas easy to see
That he had a vast resource of knowledge.
And he showed me his charts,
(The more interesting parts),
And he spoke like a teacher in college.

I was told how the highs
Brought change to the skies;
How the lows were a trifle depressive.

As he warmed to his task
I was prompted to ask
Which record he found most impressive.

It was silly, I know,
For it started a flow
Of facts - some involved, some simplistic.
And the tempo increased
As a flood was released
Of every unequalled statistic.

Record floods, river heights,
Length of days, length of nights;
Full details of every disaster.
Record rainfalls that fell,
Marble Bar's long, hot spell;
The figures came faster and faster.

For two hours and a half,
He, ignoring the staff,
Continued without hesitation.
Spoke of temperatures high,
And a twenty-year dry,
That happened at some outback station.

"Just this month," he relayed,
"A new record was made,
When for twenty-five days it was windy.
For not ever before
Had they passed twenty-four
In June, in the township of Bindi."

At last, with a cry,
And a gleam in his eye,
His manner became quite aggressive.
In a voice partly cracked,
Said, "I'll tell you a fact,
That to me is truly impressive!"

Then this last fact he spoke,
And he stifled a choke;
He was tired, near the end of his tether.
"Since our records began,"
Almost shouted the man;
"We've not had one day without weather!"

FOG

(As we sit in glorious sunshine high above the Huon Valley, we often see the valley below covered in fog.)

The fog lies heavy in the vale,
Depressing everyone.
Through the fog, a circle pale;
A cold, insipid sun.

But we, in bright autumnal glow,
Live high above the cloud
That dampens all who dwell below,
And wraps them as a shroud.

No misery to us it brings,
It is a splendid sight;
As, unconcerned, it reckless flings
The sun's reflected light.

FRESH MEAT

(As the early prospectors fossicked In the Tasmanian wilds, they would often build a small hut, a rudimentary one-roomed dwelling. The hut would be furnished with very basic bush furniture; and a fireplace would be constructed for warmth and cooking.
These hardy souls would carry in their supplies of flour, tea, and sugar; along with all the gear needed for prospecting, and stay there in isolation for periods of up to three or four months at a time.
Fresh meat was, mostly, an unheard of luxury, except for some of the more resourceful blokes, and it is about these that this poem is written).

The mining folk of earlier days
Were known for their inventive ways.
For months they'd live out on their own;
No radio, no telephone.
Their home a tiny one-roomed shack
Far off the normal beaten track.

A fire to cook and heat each night;
Perhaps a candle for some light.
Outside the hut, as like as not,
A fenced, but tiny, garden plot;
And there fresh vegetables they grew,
To supplement their meagre food.

The fence, of course, kept wildlife out,
For there was much of that about.
The miners often tried to shoot
A wallaby, or bandicoot.
But some of the more wily chaps
Devised these marvellous little traps.

In the fence they'd put a gate,
Solid, and of heavy weight,
That, window-like, would upward slide:
And to this gate a rope was tied
That connected to the hut,
From where the gate was easily shut.

The animals would turn up late
And quickly find the open gate.
Each trusting, unsuspecting beast,
Would go inside and a have a feast.
The miner, when he went to bed,
Released the rope above his head.

With gentle thud the gate would drop,
As beasts enjoyed the vegie crop.
And, when the miner rose next day,
The wallabies would have to pay:
For there, inside his garden plot,
Was fresh meat for his cooking pot!

BAG APRONS

(In years past, calico flour bags and hessian sugar bags were often converted into various household items, all of which increased the lifespan and usefulness of the original material. This is a poem about two such items).

When I mention sugar bag, I'm really thinking sugar sack,
That's how we'd buy our sugar once, not in a fancy plastic pack.
And sugar bags were used a lot to store, to carry, and to sew,
For country women used these sacks to make their aprons years ago.

Theyd cut the sack the proper shape; one piece would
  make the bib and skirt,
Making sure the length was right, and wide enough to stop the dirt.
Perhaps a worn-out dress was used, it didn't matter what the size,
And cut in strips to make the hem, and borders,
  neck-band and the ties.

They'd often add a pocket, too, and trim it nicely like the rest;
Sometimes they even added lace, and kept the apron as their best.
These bag-aprons always had the printed label facing in;
Once washed and ironed, these aprons looked as bright
  and new as any pin!

It wasn't only sugar bags, but flourbags were used as well,
But not for pretty aprons though, as many women I've heard tell:
I think that nowadays you'd see heads turned to give a
        second glance,
If underneath a skirt was glimpsed a flourbag pair of printed pants!

BUSHWALKING

(A question I am often asked is, "When do you write poetry? Do you wait for inspiration?"
The answer is both 'yes' and 'no'. In the words of one writer "If you waited for inspiration you'd never write anything." A little hard, perhaps, but with more than a grain of truth.
This poem, however, was inspired by a bushwalk I did with some mates in Tasmania's Lake St. Clair region. I actually wrote this in the notebook I always carry as I scrambled down from the top of the Acropolis, a mountain of awesome size, and even more awesome views!)

What inspires a man to climb
The mountains in the autumn-time?
Is it just because they're there?
Or for some idiotic dare?
Or just to prove one's fit enough
To complete a climb that's tough?
Each one of these, at times, is right;
But others climb for sheer delight.

Not for the joy of aching knees,
Or scrambling over fallen trees.
Not for the joy of carrying packs
That cause so many aching backs.
Not for the beads of perspiration,
But for the pure inspiration
Of living pictures unsurpassed
When one gains the peak, at last.

A city dweller cannot see
The view that lies in front of me,
As wearily I sit me down
On Acropolis's crown.
How can one describe the thrills,
As row on row of distant hills
Unfold before my very eyes
Beneath the blue autumnal skies?
And my mountain throne commands
Views of jewelled alpine tarns;
While patches of the brilliant snow
Reflect the sunlight's mystic glow.

Anxieties and troubles cease,
For here the world is all at peace.
Massive cliffs of sombre grey
Stretch towards the timeless day.
And, beyond suburban reach,
I see the golden native beech.
The photograph, and artist's paint
Give but a feeble semblance faint
Of the beauty, vast and grand,
Inherent in our glorious land.
I climb the peaks for inspiration
Of God's incredible creation.

THE CENTIPEDE

The many-legg-ed centipede is always on the run,
Always nervous, ever anxious, never having any fun.
With umpteen feet all on the move it loses its control,
And thus can never undertake a pleasant Sunday stroll!

AN OLD MATE

("The dog is man's best friend." How often have we heard that statement?
This poem was written a day or two after the loss of a dear old mate, Eli,
a faithful, full of mischief, Jack Russell terrier.)

Old Eli was a special dog, our old Jack Russell mate,
He'd been with us for fourteen years, he'd slowed a bit of late:
We've also got a little bitch, and Hannah is her name,
She was only half his size, but every bit as game.

Old Eli liked to sit inside, or potter round the garden,
And often make a dreadful smell, and never beg your pardon.
His eyesight, and his hearing, too, had long begun to fail,
But each of us he'd fondly greet, and gently wag his tail.

We could leave him safe outside, he'd never run away,
Except when Hannah stirred him up, just like the other day:
The back door had been left ajar, and, as only Hannah can,
She gathered Eli on the way, and off the duo ran.

It was mid-afternoon they left, but we weren't worried then,
For when they'd run away before they'd soon be home again.
But tea-time came, and tea-time went - the light began to fail;
We called and whistled loud and long, but all to no avail.

Now Hannah is my daughter's pet, and, all the following day,
She, with her friend went searching, calling all the way:
But not a sign of dogs they found, nor heard a distant bark,
So sadly, and with many tears, they ceased their search at dark.

Next morning still no sign of dogs; my daughter caught the plane,
Thinking that she'd never see her little dog again:
But, oh! What joy and what delight! For, late that afternoon,
Our little dog came home again, and not a jot too soon.

But what of Eli? Poor old dog, he's now been gone a week;
I reckon that he's died somewhere in scrub beside the creek.
I think that Hannah stayed with him for those two nights and days,
Until she realised he was dead, and left him where he lay.

We miss our old Jack Russell mate, the house seems emptier now,
Without our Eli's gentle snore, our Eli's ageing growl.
No longer will he trip us up, or stare with clouded eyes;
Oh! How we miss our long lost pets when any of them dies!

A WINTER'S MORNING

There's silence below in the valley, there's a patch of mist on the hill,
The cattle are peacefully sleeping, the leaves on the trees are all still.
The birds have not yet awakened, the sky in the east sombre grey;
The star of the morning is fading, as the night gently passes away.

The grass in the paddocks is covered, painted a pure, frosty white,
The houses and trees are uncoloured, grey in the pale morning light.
The snow, lying thick on the mountains, is tinged with the
    faintest of gold,
And the air is so thick you could snap it, and my nose
    blushes red in the cold.

A spiral of smoke from a chimney tells me someone is up and about,
And I say to myself, "Must be Doris - she'll be making a cuppa,
    no doubt."
I watch as the plume stretches upward, no wind to disturb it at all;
And the silence is fleetingly broken by a plover's harsh,
    chattering call.

As the pale light of dawn slowly brightens, colour replaces the grey;
And more columns of smoke I see rising as other folk
    welcome the day;
The cattles' breath steams in the paddocks, the horizon
    is broken at last:
The valley is flooded with sunshine, and the magical moment is past.

IMAGINATION?

(Another poem about the Huon Valley, the place where I live. Yet it could be about your home, or anyone who lives in peaceful rural Australia).

It might be fancy it is true
I see the sky as brighter blue;
And the valley's pastoral scene
Has a more intensive green.
The Friesian cows contrast more starkly,
And the river runs more darkly,
In this place I call my home.

The breezes blow a cleaner air
Than the urban dwellers bear.
Here nature's sweetest songs abound
Unhindered by the traffic's sound.
Here life is lived at slower pace
Than city dwellers have to face.
Farmers wave a cheery hat,
And folk have time to stop and chat,
In this place I call my home.

WHAT DO I MISS?

("Some folks likes the city, and some folks likes the country."
This is a poem of comparisons, and it shouldn't be too hard to see where my
preference lies - and, maybe, yours too!)

CHAPTER ONE

City born and city raised,
Some, I'm sure, would be amazed
To think I chose to leave the town,
And in the country settle down.

But I can truly tell you this,
There are some city things I miss.
Peak-hour traffic, blaring horns,
Sound of neighbours mowing lawns.
Shopping crowds, and dirty streets,
Buses full, no empty seats.
Flashing signs, and rowdy nights,
Pedestrian and traffic lights.
Hustle, bustle, rush and tear;
Noise and people everywhere.

Oh! There's more I miss, as well,
More than I have time to tell.
Graffitied walls, and broken glass,
Over, through, and underpass.
Concrete buildings towering high,
Hiding views of smog-filled sky.

Polluted beaches, tainted air.
And, at night, the constant glare
Of headlights, as along the road
Folk slowly drive to their abode.

"A dreary picture, bleak and grey,"
I hear my readers sadly say.
But let me cheer and hearten you,
There's better news in chapter two.

CHAPTER TWO

I love the peaceful country life,
Where I live quietly with my wife:
And, you know, we've never yearned
For the city-life we spurned.

But, nonetheless, the city had
Attractions - it's not wholly bad!
Here, with paddocks full of crops,
You won't find many corner shops!
Takeaways of every sort
Are, in the city, easily bought.
And anything you wish to buy
Is in Department stores nearby.
But not out here; and mail is late,
Especially if it's interstate.

We miss, somewhat, the latest plays,
The concerts, and the art displays.
Films and ballet, theatre, too,
Or some extravaganza new.
The city's home to first-class sport,
On cricket ground and tennis court.
So rarely do I get to catch
An Aussie Rules or Ashes match.
And, of course, no trams or trains
Run along our country lanes!

There are some positives we see
In city life - but, as for me,
I like my peaceful country place,
Far from the city's hectic pace.

TRANQUILLITY

(A short poem to emphasise our peaceful lifestyle!)

The smell of burning gum-leaves, the softly sighing breeze;
The eagle in his heaven, the gently swaying trees.
The warmth of autumn sunshine, the plover's raucous call.
The busy, bustling streamlet, and its sparkling waterfall.

The magpie's silver warble, the kookaburra's mirth;
The scent of rain that's falling upon the thirsty earth.
The sunset in the evening, the snow upon the hill,
The boobook's midnight greeting, when all the world is still.

The blossom of the wattle, the distant croak of frogs;
The sight of lizards sunning amongst the fallen logs:
Each are part and parcel of nature's soothing balm,
And give, to those who find it, tranquillity and calm.

HORSES

(Over the years I have received many requests for poems on various subjects, and one that is often asked for is a poem about horses. This has proved somewhat of a problem, for both my interest in, and knowledge of, horses is minimal, to say the least. But after much coaxing, even bullying, I came up with this!)

I've been asked to write about horses, but that's not so easy to do,
For I'm not a great expert on horses, and I've only ridden a few:
I know that one end faces forward, the one with the eyes and
      the mouth;
There's a fertiliser factory the other, the end I suppose you'd
      call south.

I've seen them in all different colours, some white, some dappled,
      some grey,
Some chestnut, some black, and some spotted, and that
      reddish-brown colour called bay.
I've heard that there's hands on them somewhere,
      although they're not easy to see,
There's sixteen or more on a biggun', but where they are
      hiding beats me!

You can ride them, or work them, or race them, and
      showjump them, too, if you're smart.
And, when I lived in the city, the milkman had one pull his cart:
And so did the butcher and baker, the greengrocer had one, as well;
The housewives would go out to meet them, and see
      what each had to sell.

If you examine his teeth very carefully, you can tell the
        age of a horse,
That's what somebody told me, but I couldn't do it, of course.
And horses need shoeing and brushing, and probably
        more care than that;
And I believe they are partial to apples, and enjoy an
        affectionate pat.

A horse can get colic, or founder; get strangles,
        pneumonia, and scours,
And other unwelcome conditions, and may need a vet within hours.
Horses can kick you and throw you, though many seem
        gentle enough,
But some that you see in rodeos are made to seem nasty and tough!

There's not that much more I can tell you, except that
        they need lots of gear,
Saddles and bridles and halters, and reins, and a bit thing to steer.
So I've written my poem about horses, and I hope that
        you've all learnt a lot;
And i doubt that I'll write you another, whether you like it or not!

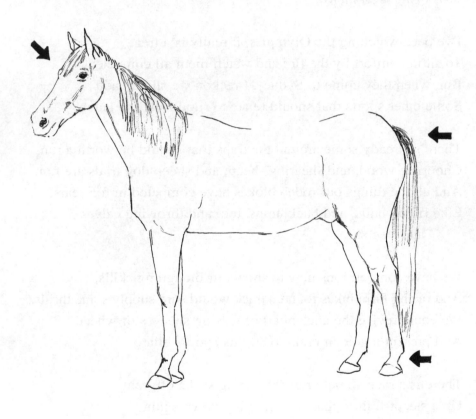

RURAL OLYMPICS

(There's a multitude of sports to watch on television nowadays, and there's more and more unusual sports being introduced into the Olympic Games. As I was watching the 1996 Games held in Atlanta, I thought that, seeing the Olympic Games are to be held in Sydney in the year 2000, I would like to see some sports which reflect much of our national character. Here are some of my suggestions).

I've been watching the Olympics, it really is a treat
To sit in comfort by the fire and watch them all compete;
But, when they come to Sydney, I reckon we should add
Some other sports that should relate to rural folk, me lad!

There's already some around the traps that should be worth a run,
Chopping wood, and shearing sheep; and sheep dog trials are fun.
And all the things our rodeo blokes have competed in for years,
Like riding bulls, and buckjumps, too, and throwing calves
      and steers.

We have competitions now to show our ploughing skills,
And racing farm bikes round a track would sure supply some thrills.
We could revive the ancient art of tossing sheaves of wheat,
And present a golden grain to all this sport's elite.

There is a race already run for carting sacks of grain
Up a steepish little road, and running down again.
Another show of mighty strength is "toss the strainer post",
Or build a haystack in an hour, and see who lifts the most.

Erect a five-strand paddock fence a hundred metres long,
With wooden posts and droppers, and strainers good and strong.
For those with some aesthetic flair, some sports we could get going,
Are synchronised hand-milking cows, or artistic paddock mowing.

Apple-picking, pruning trees, skinning rabbits, too,
Rolling drums of diesel fuel, or spinning a lasso.
All the farming things we do could make some sort of race,
Even changing tractor tyres would not be out of place.

So as I sit and watch TV I dream my little dream
About some fancy Rural Games and farming sports supreme:
I know that's all it really is, a dream, a harmless joke;
And yet I'd love to show the world the skills of country folk!

A SWARM OF BEES

(This poem could have easily been titled "The dangers of Drink", for when one has a set project in mind, a clear head is required. I was told this story by a South Australian, who is convinced it is true, having heard it from a mate who knows the 'Jack' in the poem. What do you think?)

Jack was always going to do the jobs around the house
That were requested regularly by Sue, his patient spouse;
But, somehow, things were rarely done, for Jack preferred instead
To ask a mate or two to share some drinks down in his shed.

As Sue was working in the house one fine November day,
A largish swarm of bees arrived, and seemed content to stay
Within the wall that stood between the kitchen and verandah:
Since Jack was slow in tackling them, it raised his spouse's dander!

For several weeks the bees remained, and really were a pest,
But long-wed Jack was expert at ignoring Sue's requests.
At last, exasperated, Sue gave Jack an ultimatum,
"It's either me or bees that go - I tell you, Jack, I hate 'em!"

"They've followed me about the house; they've fallen in the stew;
They've interrupted all this week the things I've gone to do.
I won't be home till evening, Jack; I'm off to town today,
If there are bees when I get back, I'll leave you straight away!"

These words he heard caused Jack to shake, he knew his wife was
        serious,
For this was no benign request, but a command imperious!
Not wishing for his wife to leave, he answered Susan's warning:
"I'll see the wretched swarm of bees is all removed this morning!"

When Susan left, Jack called his mate, "I've got a job to do;
And I'm not sure I'll get it done without some help from you."
Steve came around to help his friend, but first they had a drink.
And then he said, "It's easiest to smoke them out, I think."

They lit some old and oily rags and put them in the vent.
The acrid smoke stirred up the bees, but few, if any, went!
So Jack and Steve went to the shed to have a further think;
And, since the day was pretty warm, they had another drink!

It took a drink, or maybe three, before ideas struck.
"I know," said Steve. "We'll use the hose, they'll drown
      with any luck."
But all they did was flood the floor, and stain the kitchen wall;
They didn't drown a single bee, not a single bee at all.

Back to the shed and a drink again; then other schemes they tried:
But the bees stayed put within the wall, and not one insect died.
At last Jack thought of a clever plan, to remove the window frame,
And vacuum up the swarm of bees before his Susan came!

Late in the afternoon it was when the window frame came out;
And Steve and Jack, their hopes up high, gave an early victory
      shout!
"This plan of ours can't fail," said Steve. "These bees are soon to die."
"No doubt about it," Jack replied. "We're brilliant, you and I!

The drinks were beginning to take effect, and both were
    three parts gone
When they stuck the pipe in the swarm of bees and
    switched the vacuum on!
Then it was only a matter of time, and the bees were in the bag;
Their ploy, it seemed, had done the job far better than smoky rags!

But, 'though they were caught, the bees weren't dead,
    and the vacuum fiercely roared,
As the angry swarm kept up their din - they couldn't be ignored!
So Steve came up with the bright idea to try and gas the lot,
And down on the floor beside the stove they found the
    connecting spot.

Lying flat on the floor they pushed the hose of the vacuum
    on the pipe
That brought the gas to the stove inside, and then the time was ripe
To turn the gas and the vacuum on, and this they did with glee;
And a loud explosion rent the air, and the room was filled
    with bees!

Five minutes it was, at the very least, before the men came to
And surveyed the sad and sorry scene, and their
    consternation grew,
For the door was split, and the vacuum gone; but what
    was worst of all,
Dead bees were plastered inches thick on ceiling,
    cupboards and wall!

It was then that Susan came home from town, and their
　　knees began to knock,
But Sue, surveying the dismal scene, recovered from the shock
And laughed and laughed both loud and long at Steve,
　　and her husband, Jack;
With hair all singed, and their beards, too, and shirts
　　blown off their backs!

Jack painted the walls, and the ceiling, too, and mended
　　the kitchen door:
And the jobs to be done around the house aren't put off any more.
But, down at the pub, both he and Steve are very much ill at ease.
For someone always asks them both how to shift a swarm of bees!

THE PLATYPUS

*(In the creek below our house, I occasionally get a glimpse of one of my
favourite animals, the platypus).*

Nuzzling the creek-bed, and rarely still,
The platypus searches for food with its bill.
But, ever alert, this creature shy
Will hide at the hint of a passer-by.
To watch this unbelievable beast
Enjoying its midday invertebrate feast,
Is a pleasure few of us can share,
For platypus sightings are all too rare.

FARM SAFETY

("Out of the mouths of babes and sucklings." This poem is a cautionary tale, just to remind us of the inherent dangers in the everyday chores we do about the farm).

Our grandson's with us for a while, he comes from interstate;
A clever little bloke he is, although he's only eight.
As I'm working round the farm, or busy in the shed,
He's there beside me, watching me, or hearing what I've said.

But, worse than that, he picks me up on things I don't do right:
"Hey! Pa!" he says, "You're grinding steel, you must
        protect your sight!"
I grab the goggles off the shelf, and, with a "Thank you, son,"
I carry on, more safely, with the job I've just begun.

I used my chainsaw yesterday up in our patch of scrub,
But, just before I went up there, I saw the little cub
Come running out the farmhouse door - he called to me, "Hey! Pa!
Your earmuffs, or so Grandma says, are somewhere in the car!"

I muttered words beneath my breath, and grabbed the
        wretched things;
But then my little grandson, Ben, held up a piece of string.
"You'll need this, Pa, to tie up Jed, while driving on the track,
You know that many dogs are hurt by falling off the back."

The dog looked somewhat mystified, he'd not been tied before,
But he had fallen more than once, and pulled up rather sore.
"Oh, thank you, lad," I said to Ben, and drove off in the ute,
Thinking how the little bloke's incredibly astute.

This morning I was splitting wood, and guess who's on the go?
"Hey! Pa! You've got your slippers on, that isn't safe, you know!"
"I'll only be a minute, son; I'm taking extra care!"
And then the rotten handle broke, and caught me unaware.

So now I'm at the doctor's, and my foot is pretty crook,
He's busy putting stitches in, and I don't want to look.
But here beside me, watching all, is Ben, the know-all nipper.
"I told Pa that it wasn't safe to cut wood in his slippers!"

FIREWOOD

(Gathering firewood and storing it is an almost universal task. It takes on more importance, of course, in the cooler parts of the country, and Tasmania certainly fits that description.
Tasmanians are the best 'wood-storers' I have seen, and one of the features of the Tasmanian countryside is the huge stacks of firewood stored beside almost every country house or cottage.)

To prepare one's self for winter there's a job that must be done,
And there's no-one like Tasmanians to store firewood by the ton!
Throughout the months of summer, and throughout the autumn, too,
There's a roar around the country that I'm sure is known to you.

It's the ceaseless roar of chainsaws as the wood is gathered in;
The countryside reverberates and echoes to the din,
As trucks, and ute, and trailer are loaded up with wood;
And the woodstacks round the houses grow as every
      woodstack should.

We cut stringybark and bluegum, we cut peppermint and pine;
You all may have your favourite wood, just as I have mine.
Ten inches for the old wood stove, and sixteen for the heater;
Stacked in rows beside the fence - you'll rarely see it neater!

Some families have, or so I'm told, five years of wood in store,
And, 'though it's hard to comprehend, there's some have even more!
But I, no matter how I try, can never fill my shed,
I rarely, if I do at all, have wood six months ahead!

No matter how much wood you cut, or how much wood you buy,
It isn't really that much good unless completely dry.
But wood stacked up, or in the shed's a pleasure to behold,
For then we know we have the warmth to beat the winter's cold!

The wood we cut and split ourselves usually warms us twice:
For splitting wood and stacking it warms us through exercise!
And often, late at night, I think, ere I to bed retire,
It's one of life's great joys to sit in comfort by the fire!

CHIMNEYS

(A little bit of nonsense!)

I like watching chimneys when I'm home, or when away,
For chimneys tell us much about the weather every day,
So you'd better listen carefully to what I have to say.

The first thing that you look at is the smoke that's coming out,
If it's heading quickly north, you know there's wind about,
And, if it's winter, it'll be a bitter wind, no doubt.

But, if the smoke is drifting south, the weather should be fine,
And, when the smoke heads skywards, I think the sun will shine,
And westering smoke may signal change in these rules of mine.

If you see no smoke at all the weather's warm to hot,
Or else the people aren't at home, which is as like as not;
Or they've got a possum stuck within their chimney-pot.

If you cannot see a chimney, then it could be late at night,
And, if it's not, there's every chance the fog is thick and white;
In either case you should be home until there's better light.

There's lots more I could tell you if I only had the time
About my chimney theory, a hypothesis sublime,
But, alas, I here must end this little nonsense rhyme!

HAPPY NEW YEAR!

(Every year, I am asked to write poems about Christmas and New Year, and last year was no exception. This was written late in 1996 to welcome 1997 - a little tongue-in-cheek!)

My dog is lame, and so's my horse,
And the veterinary's out, of course:
And I discovered, just today,
A plague of mice is in my hay.
The possums have attacked my fruit,
There's far too many here to shoot!
And, because of so much rain,
The cherries have all split again!
But, though my fruit looked pretty bleak,
My grain was looking good last week:
But, when I thought the rain had stopped,
A hailstorm flattened half my crop!
My bottom paddock's still so wet,
There's no way I can spray it yet.
Footrot's rife among my ewes,
And all my cows have got the blues!
But otherwise, here on the farm,
Things are running like a charm!
So, as the old year drifts away,
There's something that I'd like to say
To all you listeners who can hear;
"A happy, prosperous New Year!"

THE OLD FARM TRUCK

(I have previously written a poem called "The Old Bedford Truck". It proved to be a highly popular poem, for many farmers seemed to have a truck like it, and related closely to it. This poem is a sequel to "The Old Bedford Truck").

I told you, once upon a time, about my ageing truck,
And how I'd have it still for years with any sort of luck.
Well, just the other day , I chanced to have a lengthy chat
With this mechanic bloke, you see, I think his name was Pat.

I'd brought my truck in to be fixed, the engine wasn't well,
It had a nasty sort of cough, and breathed an oily smell.
This Pat, he had a look at her, and said, "She's had the biscuit!
I'll have to take it all apart to have a hope to fix it!"

"This truck of yours," he says to me, is past its use-by date;
Grumbling diff., the springs are worn, the tray won't take a crate.
The gear-box, too, is nearly gone, the body's full of rust;
But you're the boss, just give the word: I'll fix it if I must!"

"Mind you, though, it won't be cheap, this engine is a brute;
The bloke who first designed it was a most sadistic coot!
Everything is back to front, and, underneath the bonnet,
There's not an inch of space to spare where one can work upon it!"

"I reckon a contortionist would find it hard enough
To reach the nuts and bolts and screws, and all the other stuff
You have to take off or undo just to start repairs,
And then, of course, this truck of yours has very pricy spares!"

"There's hardly any of them left, and, being imported, too,
You'll find that even tiny parts will cost a bob or two!
And even then I'm not that sure the parts will be on hand,
But a reconditioned motor costs, I'd say, p'raps twenty grand!"

"But if you want it fixed," he says, "I'll do it for you, mate;
Me labour's forty bucks an hour, I've got to charge that rate
Just to meet me overheads - what's that you said to me?
How long a job? At least two days, but, more than likely, three!"

I didn't get the engine fixed. I got back in my truck:
I drove it to my shed at home, and there the old girl's stuck.
I couldn't start her up again, I sadly left her there,
Knowing that she wasn't worth the cost to be repaired.

I went to town to look about to see what I could buy;
Everything I saw, I thought, was priced a-way too high.
But, regardless of the cost of them, I knew I'd need another,
And, would you know, I bought the truck from Patrick's
        younger brother!

THE COUNTRY LETTERBOX

(You'll see them along every country road, or clustered at the end of a lane, like so many teenagers hanging around after school. The country letterbox is sometimes a thing of beauty, but more often plain and utilitarian in the extreme).

RSD or RMB, it matters not the name,
For, whatever the initials, the purpose is the same.
These rural letterboxes are all along our roads,
Waiting each day to receive the country postman's load.

Now letterboxes in the town, in good or bad repair,
Have rarely any character, most seen are small and square.
But letterboxes in the bush stand large and proud and tall,
Unlike their city cousins in any way at all.

There's metal milk cans set on posts - welded, nailed, or wired;
Some are rusting badly now and need to be retired!
But others have a fresher look, painted bright and bold;
Some with folk art are adorned, a picture to behold!

There's plastic drums and metal drums, with every size in store,
From tiny, square one-gallon cans to mighty forty-fours!
Some have fancy weather-shields, and doors and locks and paint,
Some are far more simple, but all look rather quaint.

There's hand-made model houses, too, with chimneys on the top,
And some are so artistic that they make the tourists stop!
There's those, as well, quite basic, a weathered wooden box,
And, on the floor, to hold the mail, the farmer keeps some rocks.

Hollow logs and metal trunks, an ancient biscuit tin,
Anything at all will do to put the letters in.
An army ammunition box, a 'fridge that's long since new,
I've even seen a water cart that's used for letters, too!

But, no matter what the box looks like, in country or the town,
No matter what the colour is, pure white or rusty brown,
No matter where the boxes are, in valleys or on hills,
The postman never fails to bring an endless stream of bills!

THE CREEK

Chattering, bubbling, gurgling along,
The creek keeps up a continuous song:
Splashing and crashing, it drops twenty feet,
Then whispers and murmurs a melody sweet.
Approaching the rapids I hear it rejoice,
Singing aloud with euphonious voice.
Tumbling past rocks it dawdles again,
Crooning once more a gentle refrain.
As it runs out of sight by the side of a hill,
It bids me farewell with a jubilant trill.

WHAT SHOULD I DO?

(Do you ever have one of those days where there are so many jobs to do that you don't know where to begin? Here's how I solved that problem!)

I need to cut the winter's wood and stack it in the shed,
But there is fencing to be done, I should do that instead:
The forecast though's for hot north winds, a nasty fire-risk day,
And I've got grass around the house that one could cut for hay!

So I should get the lawnmower out, but first I'll spray the weeds,
For they are thick upon the drive, I don't want them to seed!
I see the drive is breaking up, I should fix that today,
For, if we get a sudden shower, the top will wash away.

A sudden downpour! That's a thought! The spouting's in a mess!
And, since we're low on water, I should fix that, I guess.
This long, hot spell, my wife just said, has made the garden dry,
And could I get some loads of mulch before the plants all die?

I suppose I should, but first I'll need to mend the broken trailer,
It hasn't been much use since Michael hit it with the baler!
But that'll mean I'll have to weld a piece back on the tractor,
For Dad backed into Peter's ute and accidentally cracked her!

So I don't know just what to do - the wood? The weeds?
        The drive?
Or weld, and fix the trailer, too, to keep the plants alive?
But now the sun is beating down - it's too hot in the shed,
I think I'll watch the Cricket Test on our TV instead!

ROAD KILLS

(An all too common sight along our country roads, the corpses of our native fauna. These bodies are a familiar sight throughout our land, but nowhere more abundant than in Tasmania).

A startled look, a sudden dash
To try and miss the impending crash;
But all too late, a sullen thump,
And yet another lifeless lump.

We race along the roads at night,
And stun the beasts with blinding light.
We don't slow down, a solid thud,
The corpse lies in a pool of blood.

Possum, 'roo, and, now and then,
Wallaby and native hen,
Bandicoot and pretty quoll
Are added to the mounting toll.

On the road all that remains
Are flattened bodies, blackened stains;
Rotting flesh, a pungent smell -
A common scene we know too well.

Is it too much to ask of us
To slow our car, or truck, or bus?
To stem the slaughter all too rife
That decimates our wildlife.

THE SKY AT NIGHT

(The sky over the city is a drab affair when compared to the star-filled sky of the distant hills).

A million stars are gleaming bright,
Silver points of brilliant light.

Unlike the washed-out city stars,
Bleached by smog and belching cars;
Pale and wan, in numbers few;
City stars are hard to view.

But here, on frosty mountain night,
The heavens are a wondrous sight:
The sky is literally ablaze
With celestial displays.

NEW NEIGHBOURS

(I wrote this poem after reading a newspaper report about city people buying up subdivided land in the country, and building their houses on these five- acre lots. Since they were still surrounded by farms, they found that all wasn't the peaceful idyll they expected, and complained about it to their local council).

Some city-dwellers, recently, have moved in next to us,
And, boy! Have they created the maximum of fuss!
Me neighbour's farm was sold, you see, and subdivided too,
And he retired up north somewhere, him, and all his crew.

I tell you, all us farmers here have suffered quite a shock,
Seeing separate houses built on each five-acre block.
Now city-folk have shifted in, to live a country life,
But, strike me! They've been stirrin' up a fair amount of strife!

You see, these city jokers, they take a Sunday trip
Out into the countryside, with all the cows and sheep.
They likes the looks of what they see, the hills all soft and green,
And thinks that they would like to join this peaceful rural scene.

But, since they've come, they've found that farms are not
    all peace and quiet,
They're whingein' to the Council that we run a flamin' riot!
"There's irrigation pumps," they say, "that run both day and night,
And cows are mooing constantly from dusk to morning light!"

When harvesting, we often work a twenty-four hour day,
But that would soon be altered if our neighbours had their way.
"We came up here for peace and quiet," and,
        stone the bloomin' crows!
They're now complainin' that the smell of farms gets up their nose!

When calves are taken from their mums, of course the
        cows will yell;
And sheep will bleat, and goats will maa, and horses
        neigh, as well.
And, as for smells, I asks ya', you'd have to be a nong,
To think that farms can operate without a little pong!

But what I fails to understand is how these city types,
When shiftin' to the country, have a bellyful of gripes
About a smell, or noise or two - I reckons that the town
Has more noise and smell pollution than a bit of farmin' ground!

But now I hears that others, the Government, in fact,
Is gettin' interested, and hopes to pass an Act
That lets us farmers run our farms with farming noise and smell,
Regardless how our neighbours whinge,
        and how our neighbours yell!

RAIN

The tanks are overflowing,
The creek's turned muddy brown,
And swiftly it is flowing
As rain still tumbles down.

The mountains are beclouded,
The heavy skies are grey:
The valley, too, is shrouded:
The rain is king today.

BULLDOG ANTS

(A poem written after having a nasty encounter with these giants of the ant kingdom!)

With fearless confidence they stride across the stony ground;
And woe betide intruders who by bulldog ants are found!
It matters not what size the foe, the ants will not take fright;
Each will defend its precinct with its own ferocious bite!

ANIMAL CLOTHING

(The colder the weather, the more likely you are to see some of the farm animals rugged up to protect them from the cold. I wrote this after seeing calves in polythene coats).

Up on the Monaro plains, and down in Tassie, too,
Sheep are often given coats to wear the winter through.
A sheet of polythene is wrapped around each woolly back,
And calves I've sometimes seen, as well,
        wrapped in these plastic macs!

Coats for little dogs are wise, especially if they're old,
And horses often wear a rug to help keep out the cold.
And, of course, we know that horses wear some metal shoes,
But I was quite amazed last week by cattle in the news.

I read that Europe recently had had a nasty flood,
And cows, in barns, stood miserably in water and in mud;
One enterprising farmer, to help his cattle there,
Made waterproof and knee-high boots for all his cows to wear!

What fashions will we hear of next - sunnies for our rams?
And woollen scarves and broad-brimmed hats for all the
        ewes and lambs?
I think a smart promoter mightn't do us any harm,
To help reduce the stockpile through "Fashions on the Farm!"

THUNDERSTORM

(I have always had a special fascination in the weather. Thunderstorms I find particularly spectacular and enthralling, as you can read here!)

The air became more humid, the wind no longer blew;
The birds all ceased their singing, and the eerie silence grew.
The sky, no longer cloudless, took on a sombre hue;
I reckoned there were thunderstorms about.

The windmill stopped its creaking - and, from behind the hill,
Enormous clouds surged upward, the northern sky to fill.
The trees stood tall and watchful, their leaves completely still,
They knew that there were thunderstorms about.

And now the dogs are nervous, the cats are all alert;
The children we have called inside, we'd hate to see them hurt:
And I, both wet and clammy, am sticking to my shirt,
There surely are some thunderstorms about.

Is that a roll of thunder? The dogs begin to bark.
The silhouetted mountains loom sinister and stark,
The early evening twilight has become unusually dark,
There has to be a thunderstorm about.

There's a dozen heavy raindrops, signalling the start
Of a crashing, raging thunderstorm - the sky is torn apart
By vivid streaks of lightning, the vision stirs my heart,
I knew there was a thunderstorm about.

The hills around are stirring, responding to the roar
Of countless peals of thunder - the rain begins to pour,
Thudding on our iron roof - I hear the rattling door
Trembling from the thunderstorm about.

And now, once more, there's silence, the sky is clear again,
The thunderstorm has moved away, as has the thudding rain.
And, through the freshened trees and air, I hear the birds' refrain:
I love it when there's thunderstorms about.

HAY

(We often hear someone pining for "the good old days".
But not all was beer and skittles back then, and some jobs around the farm
were somewhat more difficult to do. There's still plenty of chores that need
a fair amount of manual labour, but many of the activities around the farm
are made somewhat easier with the help of modern-day machinery. Hay
carting is a case in point!)

I remember, I remember,
Long ago, one mid-December,
Watching some old-fashioned farmers,
Like museum dioramas,
Slowly through a paddock creeping,
Cutting hay with scythes a-sweeping.
The grass the cutters left a-lying,
Others into sheaves were tying,
Stooking many sheaves together
In the hot December weather.

Once the hay was right for stacking,
Through the paddock I saw tracking
Horse and cart, so men could garner
All the sheaves for the ancient farmer.
Then the cart, the paddock crossing,
Took the hay where men were tossing
Sheaves, with pitchforks, through the air,
Where they were caught by others there,
And built a stack, as I've heard said,
Like some gigantic loaf of bread.

It's only sixty years, I'm guessing,
That farmers still by hand were pressing
Fresh-cut hay with home-made balers.
They'd cart the sheaves on wooden trailers,
Remove the twine, and press the grass
To form a largish bale, or truss,
One fifty pound, or somewhat higher,
And tie it up with fencing wire.
Bales like these were easily packed
Into a shed, or simply stacked.

But farmers with huge paddocks needed
Ancient methods superseded.
And now a multitude of bales
Machinery makes, and rarely fails.
Round bales, square bales, large or small,
There's now machines to make them all!
Some new balers are fantastic,
Wrap your fresh-cut hay in plastic.
You can do away with stacking
When bales are wrapped in fancy packing.

Scythes and pitchforks, stooks and sheaves;
There's not too many farmers grieve,
And wish to work the former ways,
In what we call "the good old days"!

THE SCYTHE

I like to wander in and browse about our salvage store,
Every week there's items there I haven't seen before;
Most, of course, are second-hand, and much I wouldn't need,
But some I find most interesting, most interesting indeed!

I happened in last Saturday and had a look around
At all the goods up on the shelves and lying on the ground;
Couches, tables, jugs and desks, wood, and nails and iron,
And, as I browsed, another bloke came in to do some buyin'.

He bought some horse gear that they had, some hames
    and swingle-trees,
And then he bought an ancient scythe, and that reminded me
Of days long past up on the farm when scythes were used a lot;
A skill that most have never learned, or now have long forgot!

I saw an expert use a scythe, once, many years ago,
I thought I'd try to use it too, but I was very slow.
I couldn't get the hang of it - it proved an awkward thing,
But Pat, the expert, swung the scythe with full and rhythmic swing.

A gentle swish was all I heard from each completed blow,
And there, behind him, as he worked, the grass lay in a row;
As he cut, he walked along, but, every now and then,
He'd stop to sharpen up the blade, and then move on again.

We don't see much of experts now in these machinery days,
And marvel when we see them work at Show or farm displays.
But , years ago, most farmers were, from what I hear and read,
Expert with so many tools we now no longer need.

WONDERMENT

(The more one looks at nature, the more amazing it seems.)

Gum tree seeds are little more
Than dust upon the forest floor;
Hidden from the keenest eye,
Inert they stay while weather's dry.
But warming sun and gentle rain
Breathes life into the tiny grain:
And from this microscopic ball,
Grows a forest giant tall.

CHRISTMAS CAROLS IN THE PARK

(At Christmas-time, throughout our nation, communities celebrate Christmas with their own form of "Carols by Candlelight." It is often as much a social occasion as it is a celebration, a remembrance, of the birth of Christ. In our own small community it is no different. Each year we gather at the local park and sing carols, and are entertained by some of the local talent. The Primary School usually sings a few carols, others sing, the local band plays, and I write and perform a poem I have written especially for the occasion. This was my poem for "Carols by Candlelight" in our valley in 1995.)

Christmas carols in the park,
Listening to the hungry bark
Of dogs, attracted by the smell
Of sausages and steaks done well.

Families sit upon the grass,
And round their mini-circles pass
Meat barbecued, and salt and sauce,
And salads, fresh and crisp, of course!

Chattering girls, and plover's call,
Sound of cricket bat on ball;
Chink of glasses, rowdy boys,
Add to all the friendly noise.

People working, carting seats,
Children eating tasty treats:
Oldies talking, babies crawling,
Toddlers walking, reeling, falling.

It is the place of yearly meetings,
Raucous laughter, shouted greetings;
Chats with neighbours rarely seen
Take place upon the village green.

Organisers, red of face,
Put the final things in place.
Someone taps the microphone,
Yelling loudly, "Is it on?"

Hands are clapped on deafened ears,
Mothers wipe their babies' tears:
The P.A. system's put to rights,
As dusk drifts gently into night.

A cry is heard of. "Hey! He's cute!"
As one child sees a bandicoot
Meandering across the grass.
And all, benignly, let him pass.

But had a possum ventured out,
There would have been a different shout;
Followed by, as like as not,
A loud and deadly rifle shot!

The microphone is tapped again,
And the compere tries in vain
To bring some order to the crowd,
Who carry on their gossip loud.

But then is heard above the noise
A loud, authoritative voice:
"Sit down, you lot, and stop the din;
The show is ready to begin!"

After just a little while,
The compere, with a grateful smile,
Welcomes all, on this fine night,
To Carols, here, by Candlelight.

"Light your candles, and let's begin
With 'Hark the Herald Angels Sing'.
The words are on page twenty-two,
Now come on, sing up, all of you."

Enthusiastic voices raise
The reverent words of Christmas praise;
The bandicoot turns up again,
As loud is sung the hymn's refrain.

As darkness deepens, so the light
Of candles breaks the suummer's night.
The children, fascinated, stare
At all the candles burning there.

The crowd, encouraged, sing with them
"Oh, Little Town of Bethlehem."
As singing starts, a car roars by
To words "How still we see thee lie."

The carol-singing's interspersed
With guests. A children's choir is first.
They, with gusto, sing out loud
To the all-attentive crowd.

Then the compere makes a call
For contributions from us all.
For money's needed to defray
The costs incurred along the way.

A cry goes up for Bill and Pat
To each remove their battered hat.
From hand to hand they're passed along
To hold donations from the throng.

The guests and carols come and go
For, perhaps, two hours or so.
Words are read and words are sung
That have throughout the ages rung.

Songs proclaiming Jesus' birth,
Songs extolling peace on earth;
Further words of Jesus ring,
Baby, Saviour, Lord and King.

Eventually the singing ends,
And family after family wends
Their weary way back home again;
Up street, or road, or country lane.

It's left to a remaining few
To finish off the work to do.
To move the seats, pick rubbish up,
The candle stubs, and paper cup.

The P.A. system's packed away
For further use some other day.
Some chap a child's toy retrieves;
At last, the final person leaves.

There's nothing left, just patches worn
Upon the bruised and flattened lawn.
The bandicoot comes out to see
The lights left on the Christmas tree.

So what's this Christmas Carol thing,
As all, with heavenly angels sing,
"Glory to God, and peace on earth,
Goodwill to men at Jesus' birth?"

Is it for friends, and food, and fun
We gather, as the setting sun
Throws out its final rays of light,
And ushers in the starlit night?

Perhaps we believe, as angels do,
The Christmas story through and through.
But, no matter why we came,
We'll see you all next year again!

THE MERITS OF FERRETS

(The title of this poem is a headline I saw in one of our rural newspapers.
My experiences with ferrets have never been ones to write home about, and
hence these verses!)

I was reading the paper last night after tea,
When there, with a picture, this headline I see:
"THE MERITS OF FERRETS" - it caused me to grin,
For the ferrets I knew were all creatures of sin!

They were snarling, aggressive, and ready to bite
Any chicken, or rabbit, or finger in sight.
I was told they would run up your trouser-leg, too,
There's no telling what damage a ferret might do!

I remember, one evening, we cornered at home
An enormous buck ferret that would bite to the bone!
But here, in the paper, they were talking of merits,
The good points of creatures we all know as ferrets.

"They won't bite if they're handled as youngsters," I read.
"They make good pets for kids, and are easily bred.
They come piebald or coloured, some plain white or black
And, except when they're breeding, they'll never attack."

Tell that to the fowls in the chook shed I've got,
If a ferret escaped he'd be killing the lot!
I looked up the ads. under 'livestock', and there
I could purchase some ferrets, twenty dollars a pair.

"All kinds, and good workers, each healthy and clean."
But ferrets and ferreting aren't part of my scene.
Oh! I know they kill rabbits, and I know I've got here
More rabbits than ferrets could kill in a year!

Yes, I guess I could purchase some ferrets as pets,
And buy the equipment, the boxes and nets.
But I'll put up with the rabbits all hopping about,
And wait for calici to wipe them all out!

THE SUGAR GLIDER

*(I often write a verse or two about the creatures I see around my block. One
of the prettiest of all is the sugar glider.)*

I heard a noise the other night, a high-pitched, yapping bark;
I couldn't see what made the sound, the night was very dark.

I shone my torch into the tree that grows beside the track,
And from the foliage high above two eyes reflected back.

A sugar glider, grey and white, with dark-tipped bushy tail,
Watched me as the world was lit by silver moonbeams pale.

High in the tree the glider sat, and on some blossoms dined;
A prettier creature in our bush is surely hard to find.